LEAD SHEETS
Real Key & Capo

MY SOUL AMONG LIONS · PSALMS 21-30

SONG OF THE KING

All the songs in this book are
licensed under the Creative Commons
Attribution-NonCommercial-ShareAlike 4.0
International License. To view a copy of this license,
visit http://creativecommons.org/licenses/by-nc-sa/4.0/

Published 2018 by Warhorn Media

All songs from the album *Psalms 21–30*
by My Soul Among Lions (MySoulAmongLions.com)
available from Warhorn Media

Cover design by Ben Crum
Engraving by Alex McNeilly, Josh Congrove, and Caleb Samland

Warhorn Media
2401 S Endwright Rd.
Bloomington, IN 47403
WarhornMedia.com

Lead sheets available for free download at ClearnoteSongbook.com
Recordings available for free streaming at ClearnoteSongbook.com

Printed in the United States of America
22 21 20 19 18   1 2 3 4 5

ISBN-13: 978-1-940017-20-4
ISBN-10: 1-940017-20-3

CONTENTS

PSALM 21
Song of the King   1

PSALM 22
Forsaken Me   4

PSALM 23
The Lord Is My Shepherd   16

PSALM 24
King of Glory   20

PSALM 25
Lead Me, Lord   26

PSALM 26
Vindicate Me, O Lord   32

PSALM 27
The Lord Is My Light   36

PSALM 28
Carry Me   42

PSALM 29
The Voice of God   44

PSALM 30
Mourning into Dancing   48

Song of the King
— PSALM 21 —

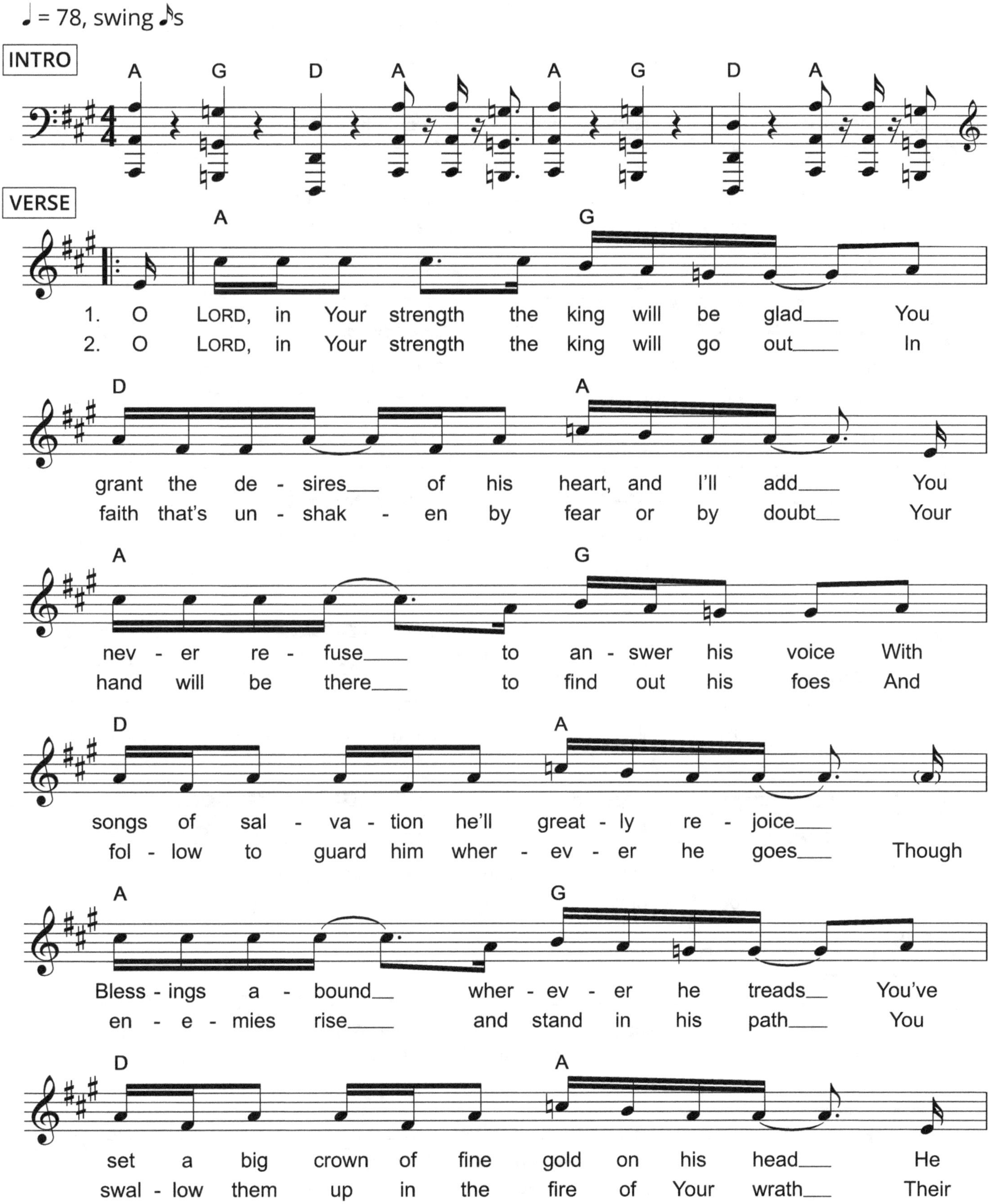

♩ = 78, swing ♪s

INTRO

VERSE

1. O LORD, in Your strength the king will be glad____ You never refuse____ to answer his voice With songs of salvation he'll greatly rejoice____ Blessings abound____ wherever he treads____ You've set a big crown of fine gold on his head____ He
2. O LORD, in Your strength the king will go out____ In faith that's unshaken by fear or by doubt____ Your hand will be there____ to find out his foes And follow to guard him wherever he goes____ Though enemies rise____ and stand in his path____ You swallow them up in the fire of Your wrath____ Their

Lyrics and music by JODY KILLINGSWORTH

Song of the King (PSALM 21) — 2

Song of the King (PSALM 21) — 3

Forsaken Me (PSALM 22) — 4
REAL KEY

Forsaken Me (PSALM 22) — 2

CAPO IV

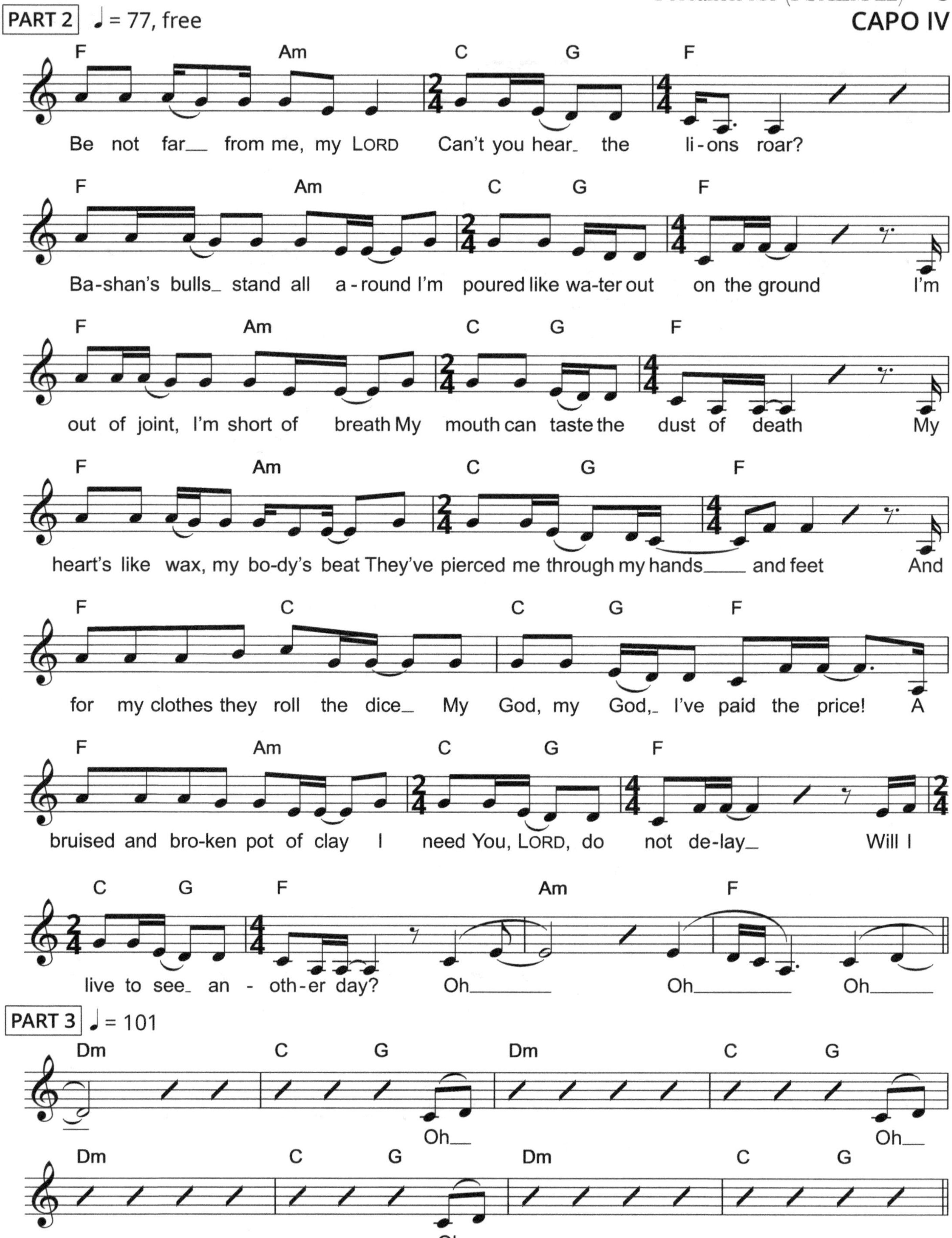

CAPO IV
PART 2
♩ = 77, free
F Am C G F
Be not far__ from me, my LORD Can't you hear_ the li-ons roar?
F Am C G F
Ba-shan's bulls_ stand all a-round I'm poured like wa-ter out on the ground I'm
F Am C G F
out of joint, I'm short of breath My mouth can taste the dust of death My
F Am C G F
heart's like wax, my bo-dy's beat They've pierced me through my hands____ and feet And
F C C G F
for my clothes they roll the dice_ My God, my God,_ I've paid the price! A
F Am C G F
bruised and bro-ken pot of clay I need You, LORD, do not de-lay_ Will I
C G F Am F
live to see_ an - oth-er day? Oh_______ Oh_______ Oh______
PART 3
♩ = 101
Dm C G Dm C G
Oh__ Oh__
Dm C G Dm C G
Oh__

The Lord Is My Shepherd
— PSALM 23 —

REAL KEY

♩ = 146

INTRO

Bb

VERSE

Bb / Eb / F / Bb

1. The Lord is my Shep-herd, there's noth-ing I lack   He
2. With God as my Shep-herd, my soul is re-stored   From
3. When to the dark val-ley of death I de-scend   I'll
4. The Lord the Good Shep-herd a ta-ble's pre-pared   For

Bb / Eb / Gm / F

makes me lie down in rich pas-tures of green___   He
path-ways of righ-teous-ness nev-er to slide___   I'm
not be a-ban-doned what-ev-er will be___   For
me in the pres-ence and sight of my foes___   It's

Bb / Eb / F / Bb

fills me with good-ness and does-n't hold___ back   I'm
held by His prom-ise, my hope is the Lord___   His
Je-sus goes with me as Shep-herd and Friend___   His
lav-ish, ex-trav-a-gant, noth-ing is spared___   My

Bb / Eb / F / Bb

led be-side___ riv-ers of wa-ters ser-ene___   Oh,
name is His bond___ and His Word is my guide___
rod and His staff___ are a com-fort to me___
head is a-noint-ed, my cup o-ver-flows___

Lyrics and music by JODY KILLINGSWORTH

MY SOUL AMONG LIONS

The LORD Is My Shepherd

— PSALM 23 —

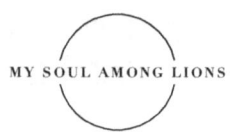

CAPO III

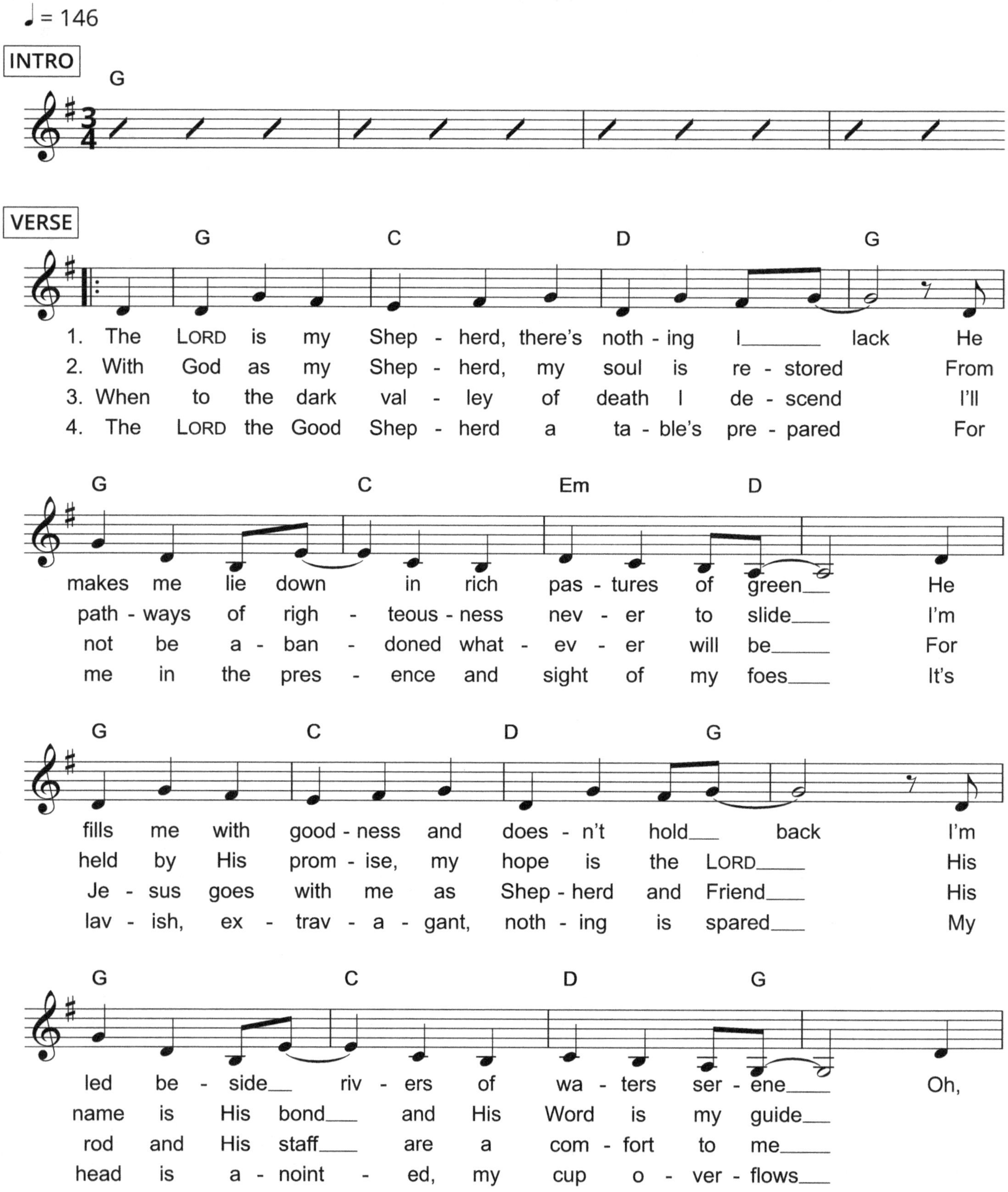
♩ = 146
INTRO
G
VERSE
G C D G
1. The LORD is my Shep - herd, there's noth - ing I___ lack He
2. With God as my Shep - herd, my soul is re - stored From
3. When to the dark val - ley of death I de - scend I'll
4. The LORD the Good Shep - herd a ta - ble's pre - pared For
G C Em D
makes me lie down in rich pas - tures of green___ He
path - ways of righ - teous - ness nev - er to slide___ I'm
not be a - ban - doned what - ev - er will be___ For
me in the pres - ence and sight of my foes___ It's
G C D G
fills me with good - ness and does - n't hold___ back I'm
held by His prom - ise, my hope is the LORD___ His
Je - sus goes with me as Shep - herd and Friend___ His
lav - ish, ex - trav - a - gant, noth - ing is spared___ My
G C D G
led be - side___ riv - ers of wa - ters ser - ene___ Oh,
name is His bond___ and His Word is my guide___
rod and His staff___ are a com - fort to me___
head is a - noint - ed, my cup o - ver - flows___

Lyrics and music by JODY KILLINGSWORTH

MY SOUL AMONG LIONS

King of Glory

— PSALM 24 —

REAL KEY

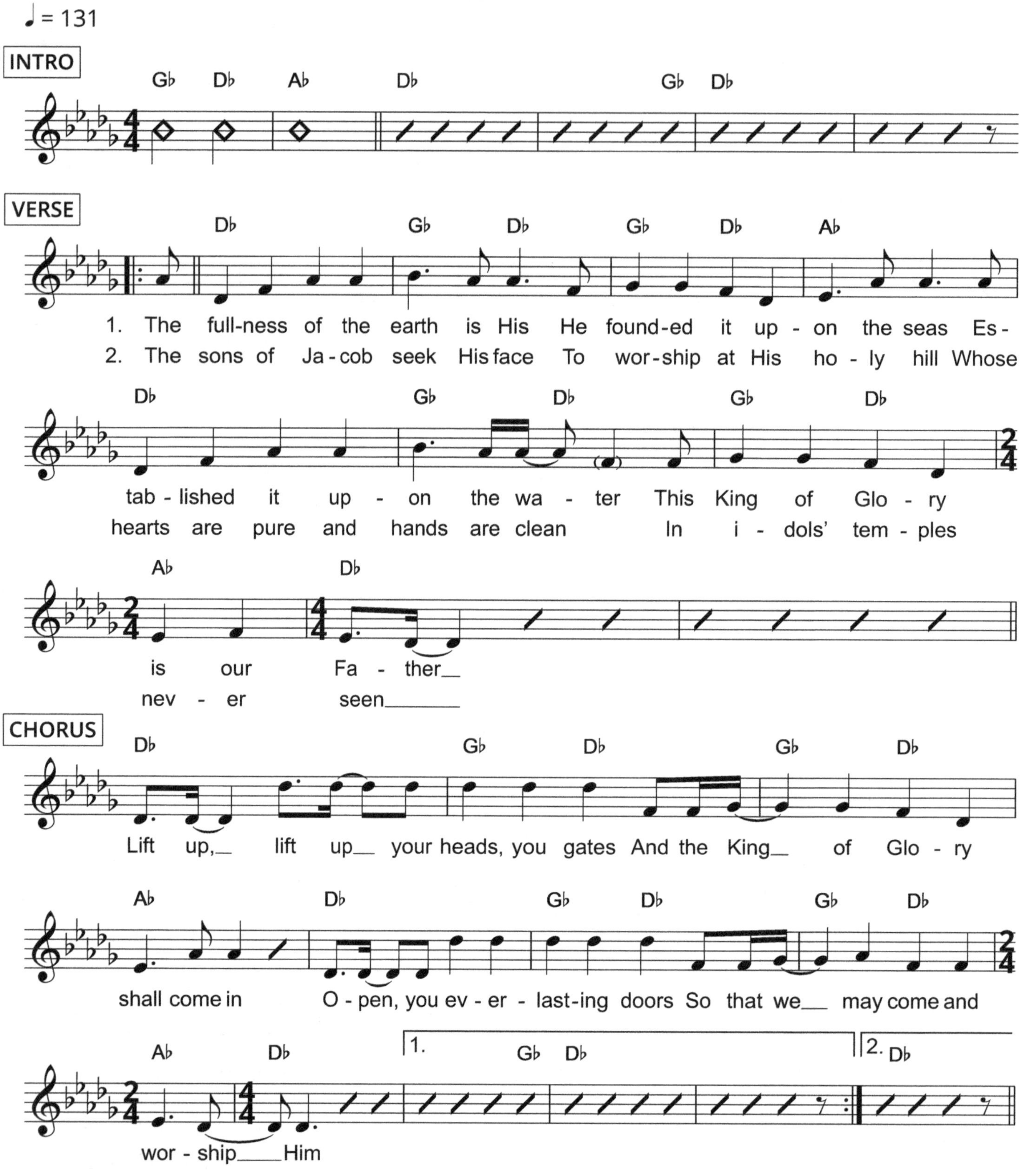
♩ = 131
INTRO
G♭ D♭ A♭ D♭ G♭ D♭
VERSE
D♭ G♭ D♭ G♭ D♭ A♭
1. The full-ness of the earth is His He found-ed it up - on the seas Es -
2. The sons of Ja - cob seek His face To wor-ship at His ho - ly hill Whose
D♭ G♭ D♭ G♭ D♭
tab - lished it up - on the wa - ter This King of Glo - ry
hearts are pure and hands are clean In i - dols' tem - ples
A♭ D♭
is our Fa - ther
nev - er seen
CHORUS
D♭ G♭ D♭ G♭ D♭
Lift up, lift up your heads, you gates And the King of Glo - ry
A♭ D♭ G♭ D♭ G♭ D♭
shall come in O - pen, you ev - er - last-ing doors So that we may come and
A♭ D♭ 1. G♭ D♭ 2. D♭
wor - ship Him

Lyrics and music by ANDREW HENRY

MY SOUL AMONG LIONS

King of Glory
— PSALM 24 —

CAPO I

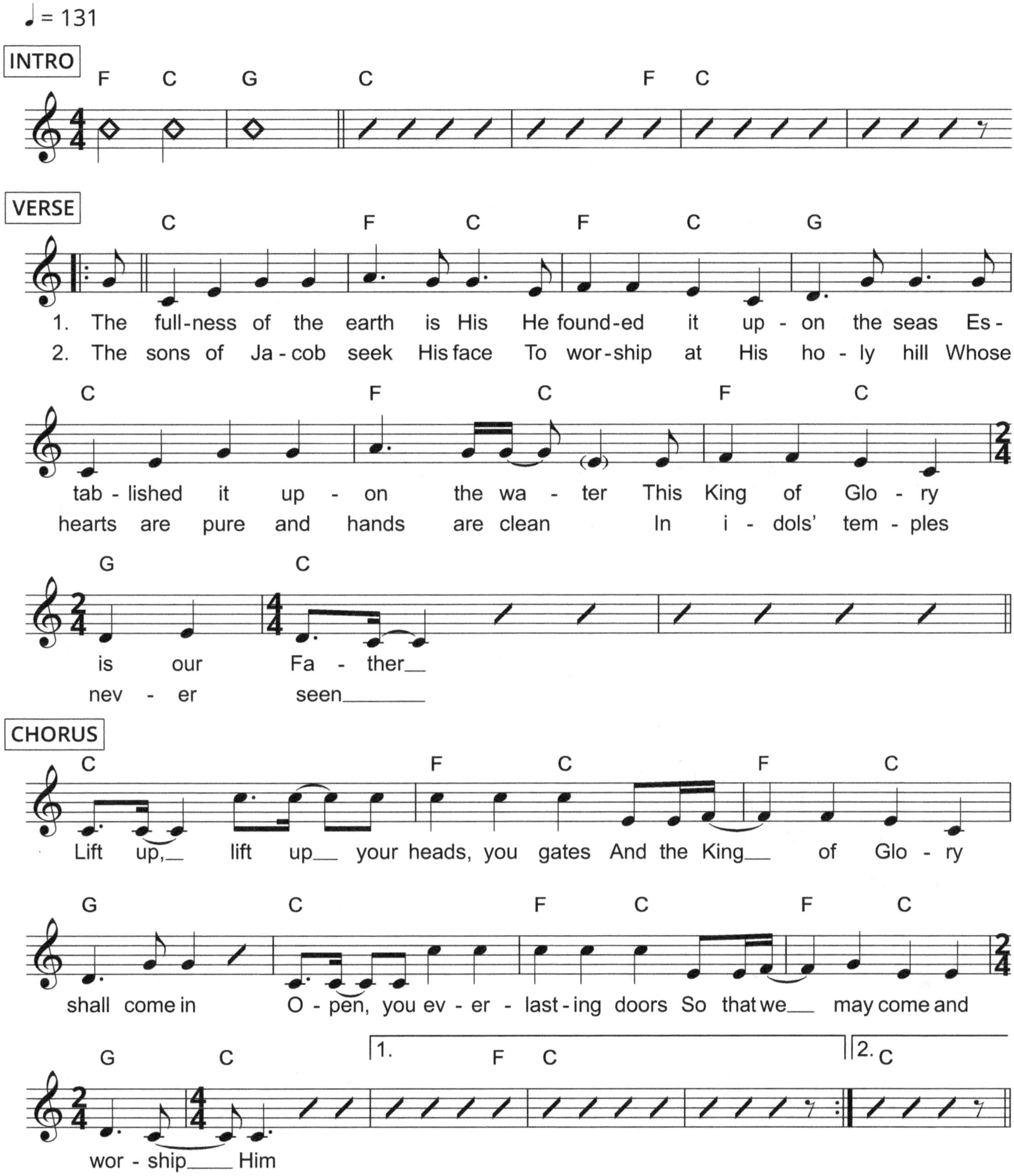
♩= 131
INTRO
F C G C F C
VERSE
C F C F C G
1. The full-ness of the earth is His He found-ed it up - on the seas Es-
2. The sons of Ja - cob seek His face To wor-ship at His ho - ly hill Whose
C F C F C
tab - lished it up - on the wa - ter This King of Glo - ry
hearts are pure and hands are clean In i - dols' tem - ples
G C
is our Fa - ther__
nev - er seen_______
CHORUS
C F C F C
Lift up,__ lift up__ your heads, you gates And the King__ of Glo - ry
G C F C F C
shall come in O - pen, you ev - er - last-ing doors So that we__ may come and
G C 1. F C 2. C
wor - ship____ Him

Lyrics and music by ANDREW HENRY

MY SOUL AMONG LIONS

Lead Me, LORD

— PSALM 25 —

REAL KEY

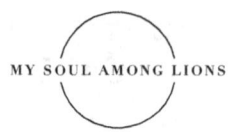

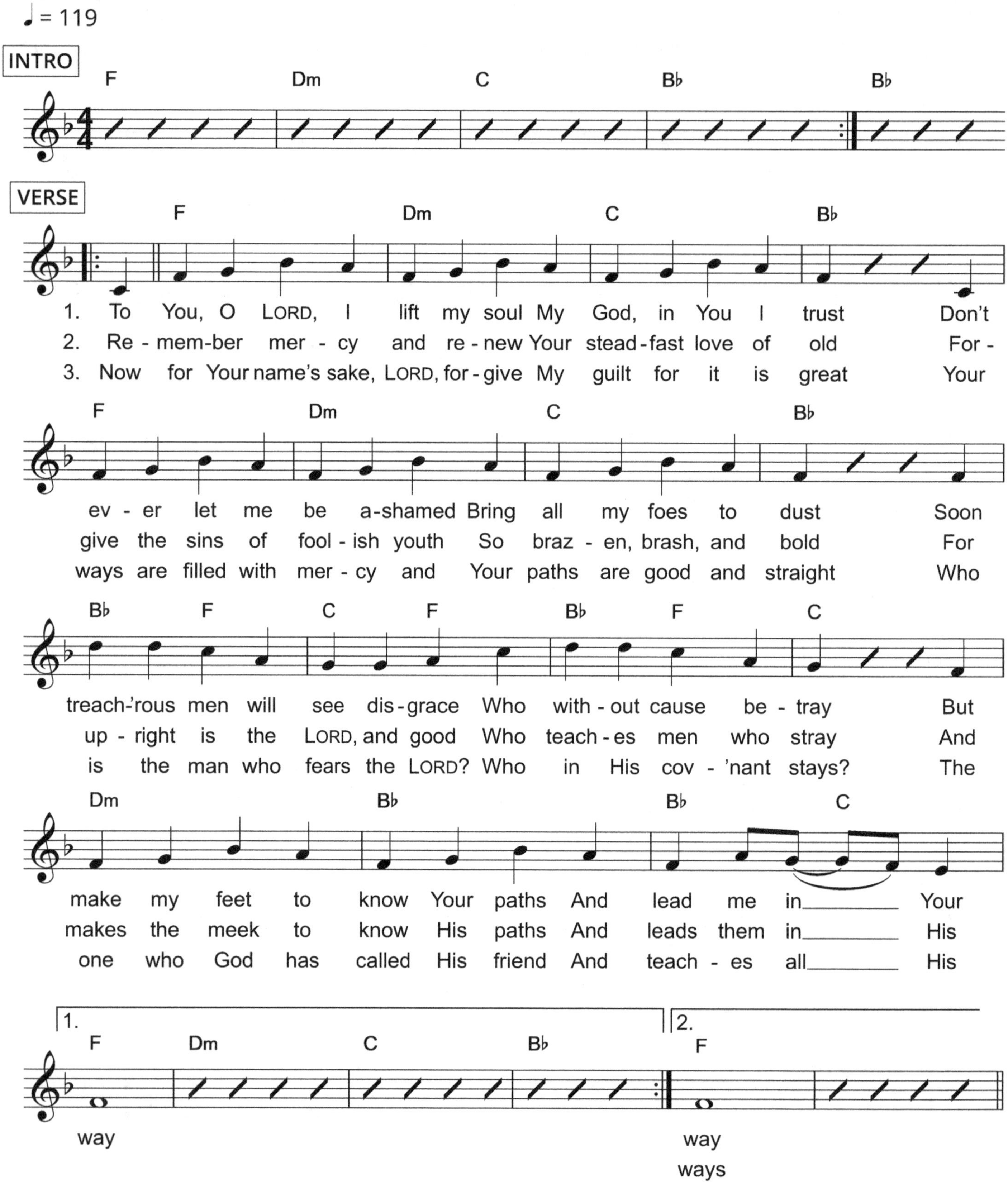

MY SOUL AMONG LIONS

Lead Me, LORD

— PSALM 25 —

CAPO V

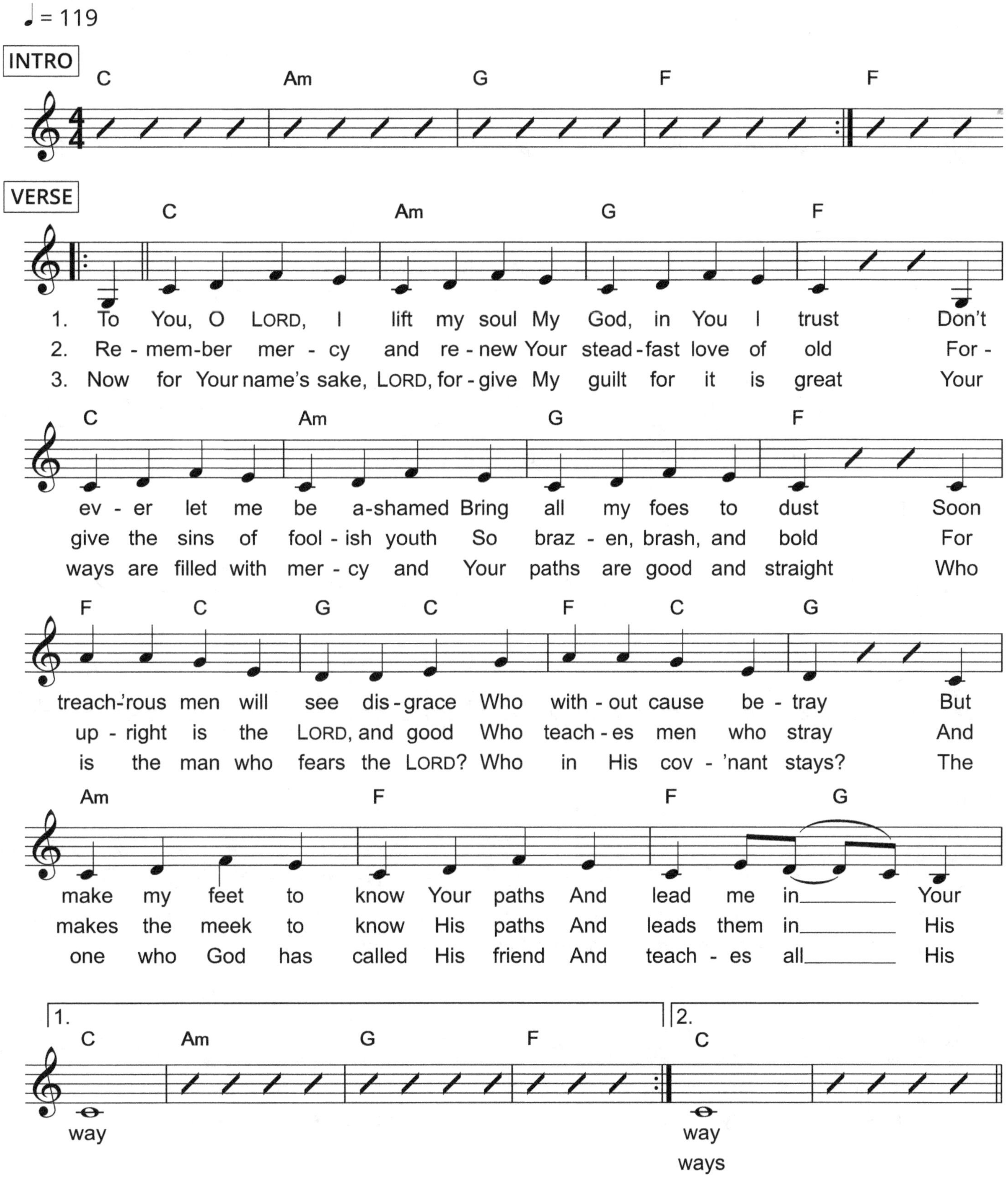

Lyrics by JODY KILLINGSWORTH and JAKE MENTZEL. Music by JODY KILLINGSWORTH.

The Lord Is My Light
— PSALM 27 —

REAL KEY

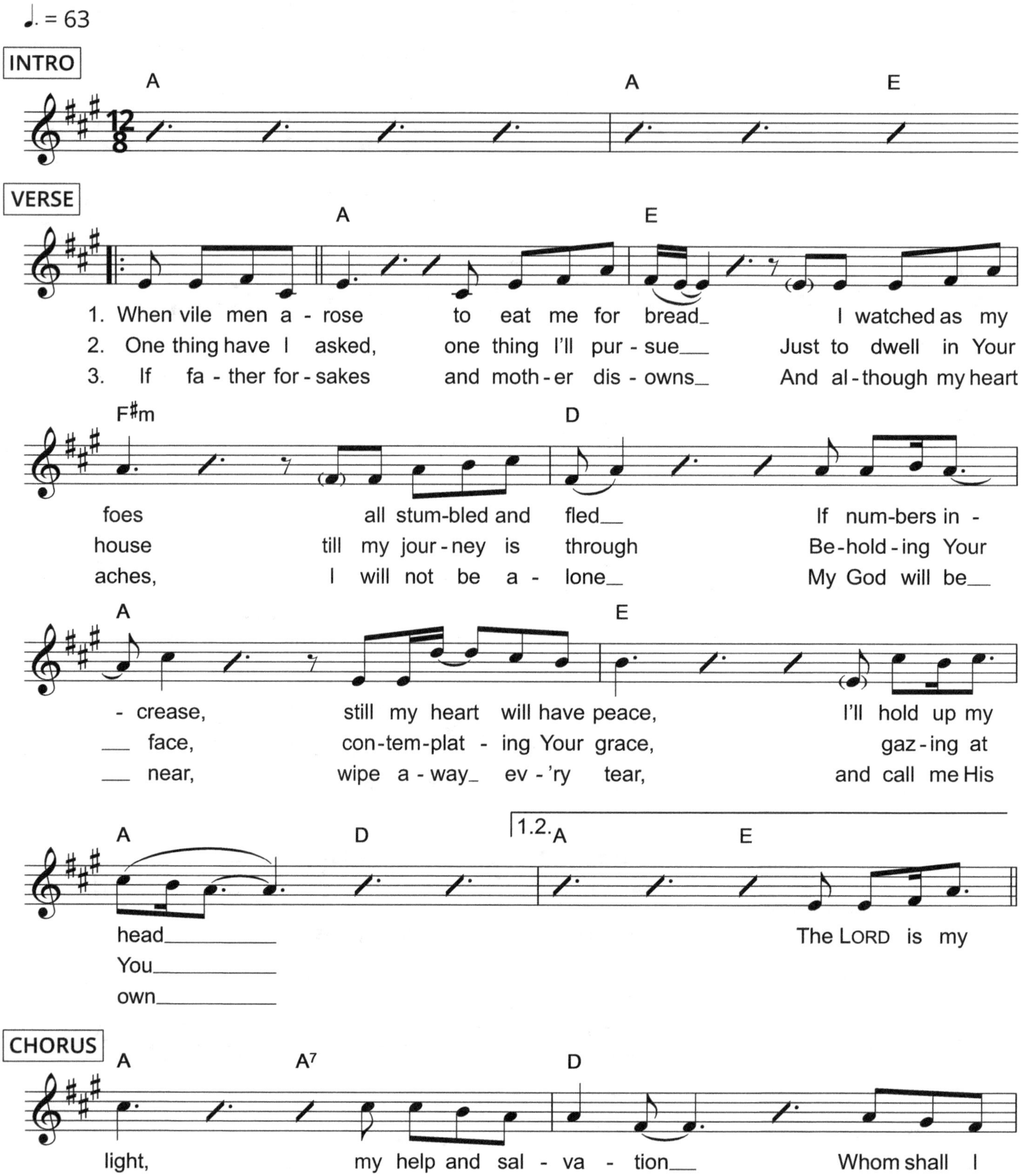

♩. = 63

INTRO
| A | A | E |

VERSE

1. When vile men a-rose to eat me for bread, I watched as my foes all stum-bled and fled. If num-bers in-crease, still my heart will have peace, I'll hold up my head.
2. One thing have I asked, one thing I'll pur-sue, Just to dwell in Your house till my jour-ney is through. Be-hold-ing Your face, con-tem-plat-ing Your grace, gaz-ing at You.
3. If fa-ther for-sakes and moth-er dis-owns, And al-though my heart aches, I will not be a-lone. My God will be near, wipe a-way ev-'ry tear, and call me His own.

The Lord is my

CHORUS

light, my help and sal-va-tion. Whom shall I

Lyrics and music by JODY KILLINGSWORTH

The Lord Is My Light (PSALM 27) — 3
REAL KEY

The Lord Is My Light
— PSALM 27 —

CAPO II

♩. = 63

INTRO | G | G | D |

VERSE

1. When vile men a-rose to eat me for bread I watched as my foes all stum-bled and fled If num-bers in-crease, still my heart will have peace, I'll hold up my head
2. One thing have I asked, one thing I'll pur-sue Just to dwell in Your house till my jour-ney is through Be-hold-ing Your face, con-tem-plat-ing Your grace, gaz-ing at You
3. If fa-ther for-sakes and moth-er dis-owns And al-though my heart aches, I will not be a-lone My God will be near, wipe a-way ev-'ry tear, and call me His own

The Lord is my

CHORUS

light, my help and sal-va-tion Whom shall I

Lyrics and music by JODY KILLINGSWORTH

Carry Me

— PSALM 28 —

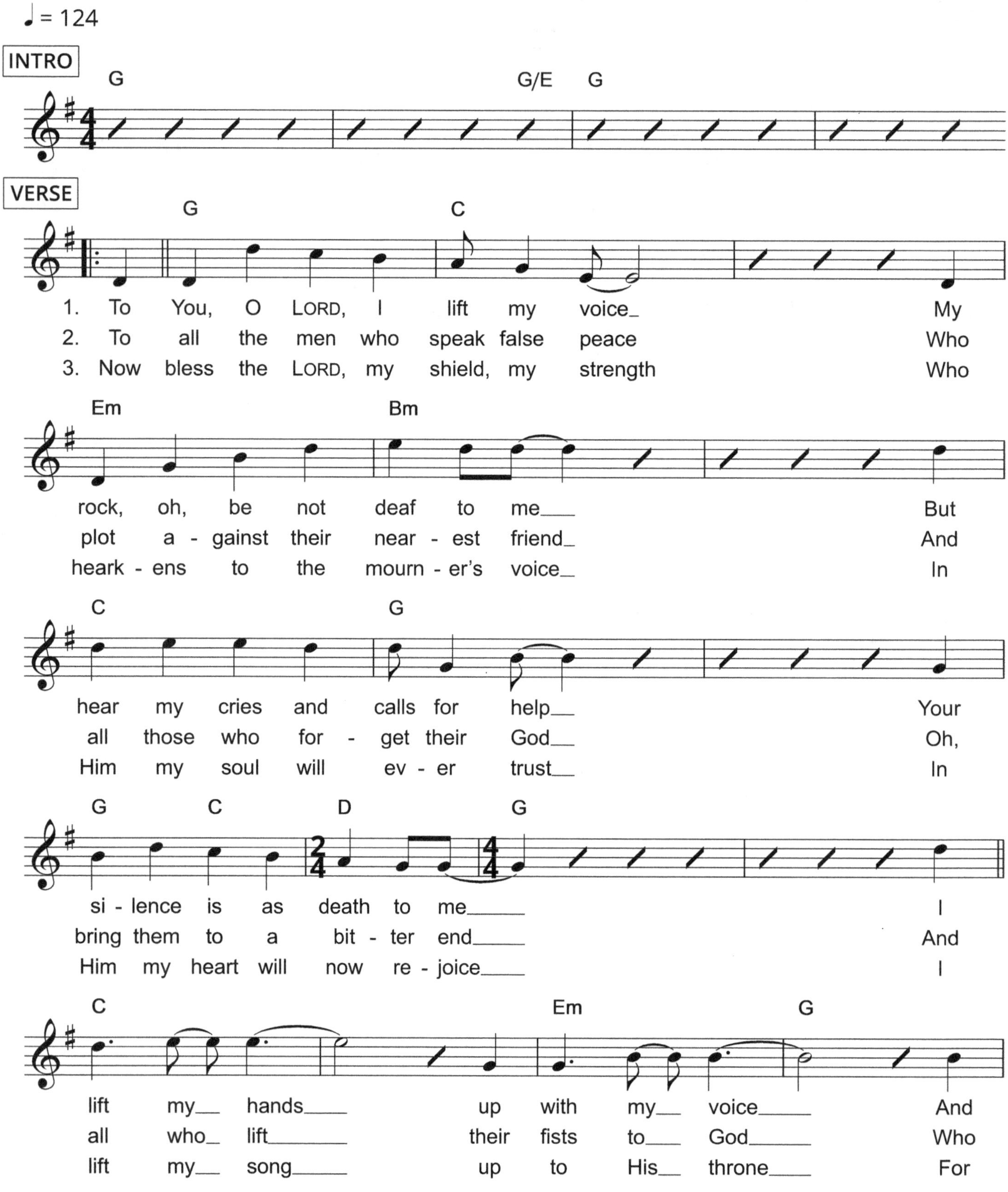

Lyrics by JAKE MENTZEL. Music by JODY KILLINGSWORTH.

MY SOUL AMONG LIONS

The Voice of God

— PSALM 29 —

REAL KEY

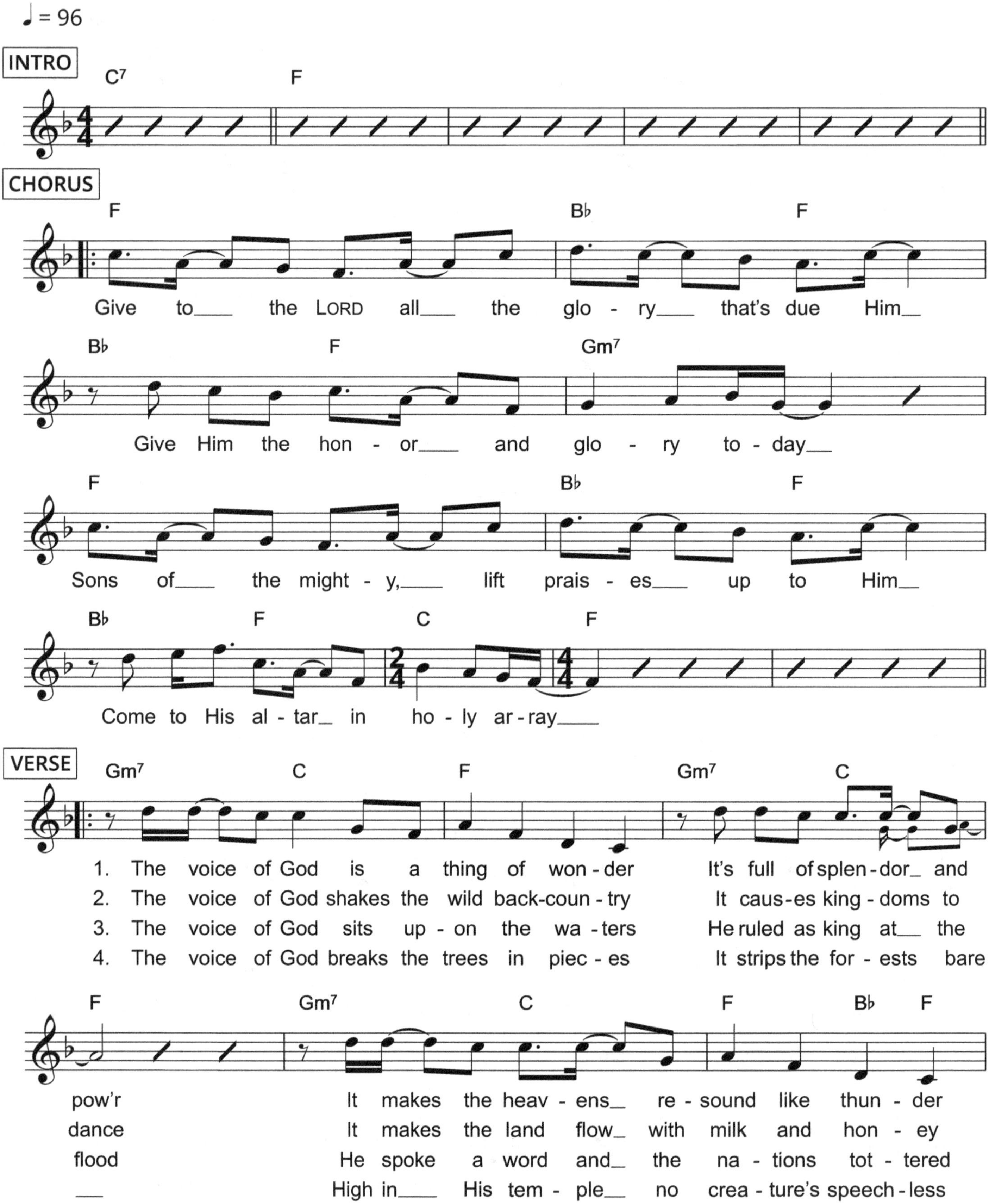

♩ = 96
INTRO
C7 F
CHORUS
F Bb F
Give to___ the LORD all___ the glo - ry___ that's due Him__
Bb F Gm7
Give Him the hon - or___ and glo - ry to - day__
F Bb F
Sons of___ the might - y,___ lift prais - es___ up to Him__
Bb F C F
Come to His al - tar_ in ho - ly ar - ray___
VERSE
Gm7 C F Gm7 C
1. The voice of God is a thing of won - der It's full of splen - dor_ and
2. The voice of God shakes the wild back-coun - try It caus - es king - doms to
3. The voice of God sits up - on the wa - ters He ruled as king at__ the
4. The voice of God breaks the trees in piec - es It strips the for - ests bare
F Gm7 C F Bb F
pow'r It makes the heav - ens_ re - sound like thun - der
dance It makes the land flow_ with milk and hon - ey
flood He spoke a word and_ the na - tions tot - tered
___ High in___ His tem - ple_ no crea - ture's speech - less

Lyrics and music by JODY KILLINGSWORTH

REAL KEY

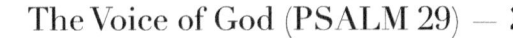

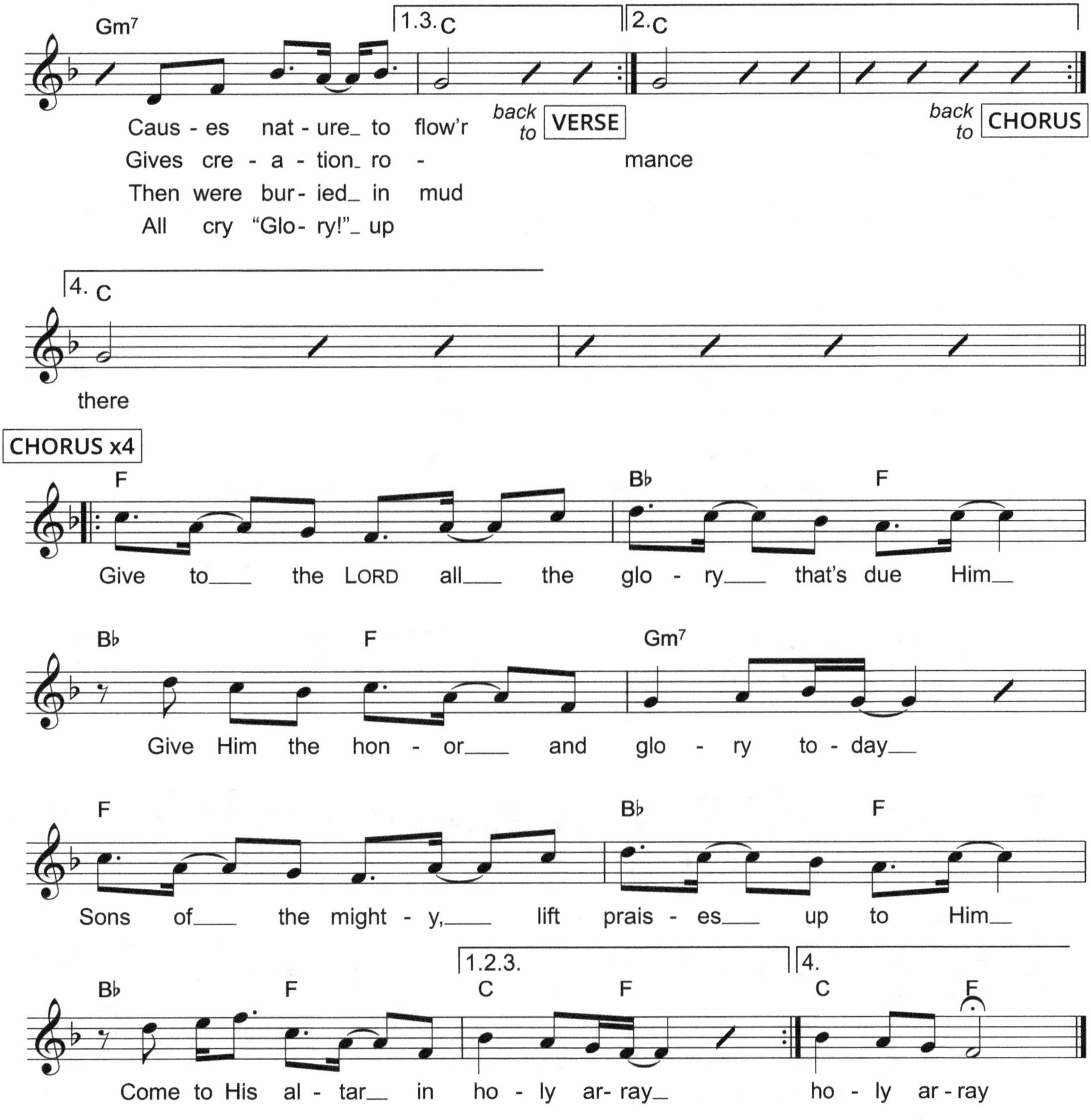
Gm7
1.3. C
2. C
Caus - es nat - ure_ to flow'r
back to VERSE
back to CHORUS
Gives cre - a - tion_ ro - mance
Then were bur - ied_ in mud
All cry "Glo - ry!"_ up
4. C
there
CHORUS x4
F
B♭
F
Give to___ the LORD all___ the glo - ry___ that's due Him__
B♭
F
Gm7
Give Him the hon - or___ and glo - ry to - day__
F
B♭
F
Sons of___ the might - y,___ lift prais - es___ up to Him__
1.2.3.
4.
B♭
F
C
F
C
F
Come to His al - tar__ in ho - ly ar - ray__ ho - ly ar - ray

Mourning into Dancing
— PSALM 30 —

REAL KEY

♩ = 114

INTRO | G F C | G F C :|| F C G |

VERSE

G / C / Am / D
I'll give you praise, O God__ For You have heard my voice____ And
When all was good and well__ I said, "I won't be moved!"__ But

G F C / Am / D
lift-ed me a-bove__ my foes_ so that none of them__ re-joice__ My
then You hid__ Your face__ a while and I quick-ly changed my tune__ I

G / C / Am / D
soul was good as dead____ I could not have sur-vived__ You
cried, "What good's my blood?__ If I go to__ my grave__ Shall

G F C / Am
reached your hand in-to the pit and You brought me out__ a-live__
dust de-clare Your praise, O God? Will it tell how You__ can save?"

D / F / Dsus / D
__ Now my spir-its You__ re-vive____
__ Here's the an-swer that__ You gave:__

CHORUS

G / F / C / F C G / F
You turned my mourn-ing in-to danc-ing Though I went weep-ing in the night

Lyrics and music by JODY KILLINGSWORTH